Healing
Through
Adversity

A DOCTOR'S TRIUMPH OVER POLIO

Healing

Through

Adversity

A DOCTOR'S TRIUMPH OVER POLIO

DR. SUNITA DODANI

Kravitz & Sons
INNOVATORS IN PUBLISHING, MARKETING AND ADVERTISING

Kravitz and Sons LLC
204 E Arlington Blvd. Suite B
Greenville, NC 27858

Published by Kravitz and Sons LLC.

ISBN: 979-8-89639-611-6 (sc)
ISBN: 979-8-89639-610-9 (e)

Library of Congress Control Number: 2025927600

Table Of Contents

Preface

According to the World Bank on April 3, 2023, 15 percent or one billion people in the world "experience some form of disability" (Disability Inclusion Overview (worldbank.org). "Persons with disabilities are more likely to experience adverse socioeconomic outcomes such as less education, poorer health outcomes, lower levels of employment, and higher poverty rates."

In a March 7, 2023, Fact Sheet, the World Health Organization (WHO) reported that "Health inequities arise from unfair conditions faced by persons with disabilities, including stigma, discrimination, poverty, exclusion from education and employment, and barriers faced in the health system itself."

The World Population Review published "Countries with Polio 2024", which indicates the following:

Since 1988, global poliovirus cases have fallen by 99.9%, and only one of the original three types of wild poliovirus (WPV1) remains in circulation. Today, polio is endemic in only two of the world's countries: Afghanistan and Pakistan. Even in these locations, aggressive vaccination efforts have dropped the number of cases to a handful a year. That said, both these countries and many others, particularly in Africa and Asia, are still vulnerable to outbreaks if the disease is accidentally introduced by international travelers or some other means." ("Countries with Polio 2024" worldpopulationreview. com)

The world is becoming more aware of the impact of disabilities in global society. Leading health organizations and many developing nations are taking steps to address the inequities and difficulties facing people with disabilities today. With awareness comes hope followed by action that will provide necessary accommodations to give everyone an equal opportunity for quality health services, education, and employment along with protection against abuse and discrimination.

I am one of the fortunate ones whose parents supported me through my health issues with polio and provided me with the means to attend school and eventually earn a medical degree. I have experienced disability first-hand and share my experience in this book to help others who face similar challenges.

First, my family is the reason for my success. Without their hard work and support, I could not have achieved all I have in becoming a cardiologist. I also thank my husband for his understanding and help with my studies and career. Everyone with or without a disability can benefit from a caring support system of family and friends who believe in your goals and will help you attain them.

I encourage readers to persevere in their quest for success, whatever form that may take. Never give up and gratefully accept the help and support that are offered.

Acknowledgments

This book is dedicated to my parents first, then my siblings, my teachers, and many friends and colleagues.

Throughout my polio diagnosis, treatment, and recovery, my parents were with me every step of the way. They facilitated my education and encouraged me to have faith that I could meet my goals and become successful.

My brothers and sister helped in many ways with my medical treatments and education, providing companionship and guidance with school homework and medical concerns.

My teachers encouraged me to do my best in school and in adjusting to student life with polio.

Many good friends and special colleagues offered acceptance, support, and mentoring at each stage of my academic career and professional development.

My husband and son have been my steadfast family inspirations. Everyone needs a solid support system. I have been blessed with many loving and kind people who believed in me and encouraged me to believe in myself.

CHAPTER ONE

Childhood Interrupted: My Fight With Polio

By any measure applied to my birth, I should not have survived. The odds of my becoming a successful physician were off the chart. How do some people struggling with severe challenges somehow manage to overcome them and achieve their dreams while others with numerous advantages fail to reach their goals?

Have you ever encountered someone grappling with life's challenges? Perhaps you've crossed paths with individuals born into the world with congenital health complications, or those entangled in families lacking crucial support systems. Others find themselves ensnared in cultures that ostracize or discriminate against them. Fortunately for the world and society at large, determined persons will not be defined or restricted by their limitations. Methodically and persistently, they take one trembling step at a time followed by another – and another – assisted by a loving family member or a dedicated caregiver. Soon, they are walking steadily, unassisted, and their stride becomes confident as they overcome one challenge after another and eventually reach or exceed their potential.

All it took was the support and encouragement of someone who believed in them.

That is the purpose of sharing my life story in this book. I want to inspire readers to believe in themselves and never surrender their quest for success.

First, I will explain the backdrop to my story to give you a clearer picture of my circumstances.

Today, in the early twenty-first century, regional conflicts are common around the world. Nations like Russia and Israel dominate the news headlines. But in the mid-twentieth century, developing countries were waging nationalist wars to establish independence and sovereignty. My homeland was one of them.

Before 1947, India and Pakistan were one country. Due to significant religious conflicts, they separated. Their respective leaders decided that most Hindus would reside in India while Muslims would populate Pakistan. (Ironically, there are more Muslims in India than in Pakistan.) Following this development, most Hindus left Pakistan. Leaving all their assets, belongings, homes, and land, they settled in India.

Our family is Hindu. We are members of a group of minorities residing in Pakistan. My father's and mother's families lived close to the Arabian Sea, so they decided to stay in Pakistan, whereas most of the other Hindus moved to India. My father came from a poor background. My mother's family, however, had a little more money than my father's, and she would be considered lower-middle class. They lived in different cities while growing up and did not know each other until they were married.

My grandfather on my father's side was a farmer, and he was the head of a large family. Their home, which was in rural Pakistan, included his father, his two cousins, his wife, and his siblings. Eventually, my grandmother on my father's side died, and my grandfather remarried. The second wife of my grandfather did not treat my father well, but despite this, my father remained humble and helped the family with his share of work without complaint.

My father was passionate about studying, which was a rare circumstance among his relatives. He was the only one in his household who rose to the social level that he did with a passion for education, and he earned a master's degree in engineering. His goal was to obtain a government position even though many doubters warned him the government was run by Muslims; a Hindu working in the government would cause controversy. Despite this, my father continued to pursue his dream of a government job.

My parents were matched through an arranged marriage. Arranged marriages are common in our community; even my marriage is arranged, which we'll get into later in the book. When they married, my father was seventeen, and my mother was twelve. It was at this time that he decided to move to a bigger city away from his family. He and my mother relocated to Karachi, Pakistan, where he continued his studies and found employment. After a period of working, he pursued his dream of entering the Pakistan government, and after years of service, he retired as the Secretary of Health, Science, & Technology. I cannot put into words how proud I am of his achievements and rising to that level despite the doubts and troubles he experienced early on.

At first in their marriage, my parents didn't buy a house. A government employee's salary wasn't much, but the benefits offered supplemental advantages. As early as I can remember, we had a government car with a driver. Government jobs also provide employees with a house, based on their rank. Years later, when my brother got a job, our parents were finally able to buy a home in 1991. My father would travel from one place to another as his post changed, so I always saw him coming and going. Despite that, he kept the family in one place - Karachi. We never moved around with him. My father was enthusiastic about our education. As children, we never had a television. He would tell us his income was spent on tuition fees or books for us to learn.

I am the fourth of my parents' five children. My oldest brother, Suresh, is now almost sixty, and he still resides in Karachi, Pakistan. He is married with two daughters. My oldest sister, Sarla, was educated in public school and went into medicine as a gynecologist. She was married in Pakistan and is now settled in Dubai with two children. The third sibling is my brother Roopkumar (Roop), with whom I am the closest. Sometimes he would accompany our father from post to post. For education, he was enrolled in a boarding school. A day came when he decided to earn a computer science degree in the U.S.

The education landscape in Pakistan stands in stark contrast to that of the U.S. Schools in Pakistan typically encompass grades one through ten, followed by the transition to college during the eleventh and twelfth years. Beyond this, students embark on their chosen career paths. (For instance, my academic journey led me to pursue medicine for a five-year duration.)

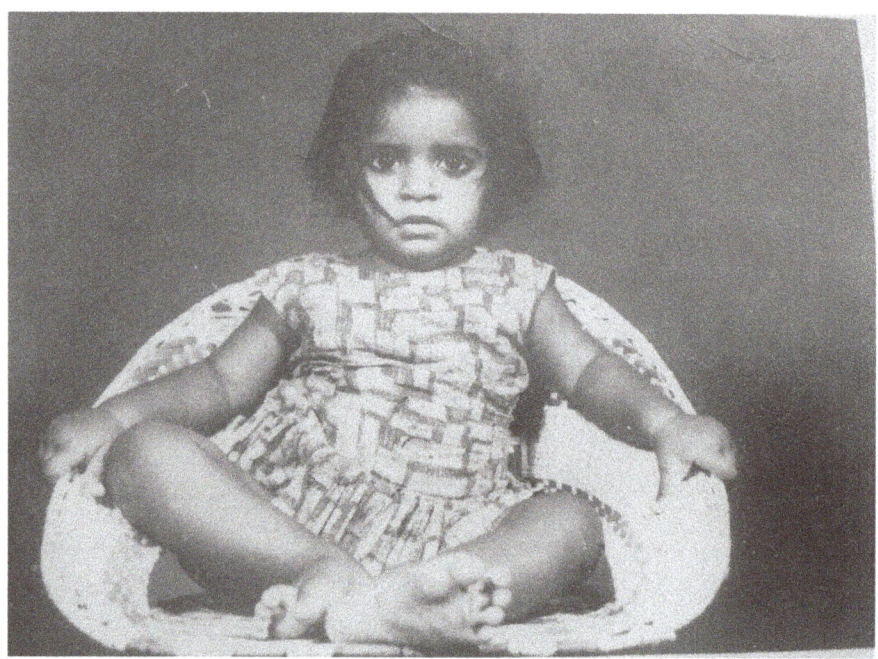

Two-year old Sunita Dodani (without polio)

I was born in Karachi, Pakistan, as a healthy baby. Most babies in Pakistan are born at home, as we don't go to the hospital for childbirth. I was born a healthy, chubby child. As I grew, I became known as a highly active child. At the age of eight months, I started walking. I could not sit still. Everyone would tell my mother, "This child is going to be a problem because she's so active!" Whenever I remember these words, I have to laugh. Our housekeeper (who came with my father's job) would take us to the park to help with my active personality.

I was an authoritative child as well, which I believe continued to develop into my adult years. My mother would often tell stories of how I would slap my older brother or older sister. I had quite a temper as a child. Imagine a one-year-old making her older siblings behave like a horse to be ridden! That was me. Family members described me as a "born leader."

"I want to go to school!" I frequently told my parents. I was so excited to learn and would often feel jealous watching my older siblings taking the bus, and I couldn't wait to join them. To help me feel included, my mother would give me almost a school itinerary; for example, I would eat lunch at noon to feel like I was in school. I had many neighborhood friends and loved talking to everyone.

Few middle-class families would get vaccinated at that time, and it wasn't because we didn't know about it. Vaccination announcements appeared on the television, but as we didn't have a television until I was nine years old, so we would sometimes watch our neighbor's television. The vaccination didn't seem especially important. But up until my father's death, he said my polio diagnosis was his fault. If he had just vaccinated me, my life would have been quite different. However, I told him my illness was my destiny. How I am now is how it was destined.

The day I became afflicted with polio, I was two years of age. I was such a naughty, hyper child. My mother later explained that I was playing with my toys on the bed and wanted to get up. But when I got out of bed, I fell. My mother thought I did it on purpose because of my behavior, so she asked, "What are you doing?" Four times she asked this and put me back on the bed. Four times I got off the bed to try to walk and fell again. I kept mumbling, "I can't walk." Polio has no pain. When she realized I was telling the truth, she called my father and took me to see a doctor. After an exam and some tests, the doctor announced I had polio, and it was affecting all four of my limbs. My right leg was affected the most.

Understandably, my whole family was shocked. My grandparents and my uncles who lived with us couldn't believe what had happened. The little girl who was hyperactive one day just wasn't mobile anymore. At first, many tests and procedures were done, both medical and others, to try and heal me. For three or four months, my parents were told, "If you give her this medicine or solution, she'll be healed!" The solutions were some of the worst things I had ever tasted. Of course, they didn't help.

Afflicted with an incurable disease and living as a minority in Pakistan, this was just the beginning of my long journey to find out who I am and what I am supposed to do.

Chapter Two

Battling Barriers: My Quest for Education

A supportive family can make the difference between success and failure. My mom was uneducated. She came from a small town in rural Pakistan, the only sister among three brothers. Yet, in a male-dominated society, her father, my grandfather, supported her as an equal to her brothers.

My dad was seven or eight years old when his mother died, and his father remarried. Sadly, the stepmother didn't treat my father well. She hardly spoke to him – only if she needed money. Compared to other aunts and uncles, my father was a little better off. My uncle – the stepbrother of my father – was different; he stayed with us and loved us. The others did not. That could be a reason my mother's role as the only girl among three boys helped her develop important abilities. She stood up for me although she became submissive when she married. Coming from a culture where women are treated poorly and considered second-rate citizens, after marriage, their sole job is to raise kids, cook, care for extended family, and do housework. Many families do not support female education; girls must pursue it individually if they can. The culture is improving nowadays for middle-class women. For those from families like ours who are minorities in Pakistan, a daughter with a disability has few options.

I don't have much recollection of when I was only two years old, but this is what my parents used to tell me about when I got polio. Certainly, everyone was in shock because all four of my limbs were affected. In the last chapter, I mentioned that I was a highly active child, but imagine a child who was so active at such a youthful age, and suddenly that child becomes completely disabled. The child cannot even sit properly because of muscle weakness.

My mother and father used to tell me that I would frequently cry. All the time. After a medical evaluation, my parents felt disbelief when the doctor told them I had contracted polio. It is a virus that invades the muscular sections of the body and affects the nerves that supply the muscles. On a diagnostic scale, I had weakness to the level of power plus-one in both legs with less weakness in my arms and zero power around my knee muscles, i.e., there is no mobility. A score of one means there is a flicker of movement, and five represents normal people with full strength moving against gravity. So, in my case, the score was plus-one, which means there was some ability, but I couldn't move without the help of gravity. My arms were a little better, but there were still problems with weakness. When the doctor advised my mom and dad to get the rest of their children vaccinated, they obeyed quickly. No one had been vaccinated, so it was a good thing they decided to do this.

During the first few months, once the news was disclosed, disbelief was paramount. This was mostly evidenced among my relatives and extended family - uncles, aunts, and grandparents. Everyone wanted to believe it wasn't true. The doctors said, "Take her somewhere and get help." For the first six or seven months, there wasn't any local medical treatment. I was taken to tombs and temples for prayers and worship. Anyone we met might give advice or share their views, including the belief that my condition resulted from black magic. It was believed someone had cursed me with a hex that could only be removed by performing three or four days of ritual practice, or so my brother told me.

Mom was the one who emphasized starting physiotherapy because that was what the doctor was recommending as the proper treatment. Her decision became a memorable life lesson: A mother is so important. This is part of my message to everyone. Those who have mothers, please keep them safe, value them, and respect them. Whatever I am today is because of my mother's care. My father likewise supported me. However, Mom was the one who stood up whenever there was a need and got things done.

When people say education is important, yes, that's true. But it is not the only bridge to success. My mother never went to school, and she came from a background where females don't even speak in the house. They are only taught to do the house chores. But moms play a highly valuable role in the home and in raising children. When my mother insisted that we follow the doctor's guidance and take me to physiotherapy, my father gave up his job because he was in shock and desperate to help me improve. He left an exceptionally good government post to give full attention to me. Despite being a member of the Hindu minority community in Pakistan's Muslim culture, my father was respected and acknowledged as an honest man. His coworkers understood why he had to leave when they learned his daughter had polio.

My older brother suggested if our dad left his government position, he would be able to obtain part-time work. This was essential since our father was the only breadwinner earning income to feed all of us as we didn't have any savings. At about six years of age, I recall witnessing my mother's distress because my father left his government position. Unfortunately, he lost not only a stable income but also supplemental incentives, like domestic help and a vehicle driver, which supported our day-to-day activities.

My family made my health a priority. Soon, my parents were taking me to the doctor routinely. Initially, the visits occurred weekly. At night, my mom supplemented my medical care by massaging my legs and arms with oils.

I was still aggressive, even if I didn't have much strength or mobility. I did not understand what had happened. I kept trying to get out of bed and walk – even though I couldn't. My brother later told me that I would always say, "I want to get out," and later, "What is happening?" While polio can affect all muscles of the body and organs, thankfully, only my limbs were affected. My lungs, along with the spinal muscles and all other organs, were fine. I could roll around on the bed, but sometimes, while rolling, I fell off the bed. My brother reminded me that I kept falling because I didn't listen, and I was so stubborn!

At age five, when the doctor gave me a full brace for my right leg and a short left-leg brace, it reached only to the knee for support.

"As she starts to walk and move around, her strength will increase," the doctor said.

I might regain strength in the left leg, but my right leg needed a complete assistive brace called a KAFO (knee, ankle, and foot orthosis). Even today I wear the full brace on my right leg because the glute muscles, the buttocks, are still weak. My right leg required a full brace, and in Pakistan, the braces were made from steel and are very heavy. It took time to get used to it.

Our home was like any lower-middle-class house. My oldest brother, Suresh, was six years older. When I was two, he was eight and going to school. My sister Sarla is five years older, followed by my other brother, Roop, who is just a year older. My last brother, Aneel, is six years younger and wasn't born yet. My two older siblings were attending school when I contracted polio. Unfortunately, our grandparents objected to the time my parents devoted to my care. My step-grandmother would tell Mom to let me be and pay attention to the house and the other kids. Thankfully, Mom wouldn't listen to that advice.

Due to our culture, my step-grandmother lived with us most of the time and did not do anything, nor help my mom with house chores. It was understood that my mother had to place the meals in front of her, and she would eat without doing anything to help. My step-grandmother didn't assist with the house or care for the children; she had no responsibilities.

When I started school, my mother was the one sweeping and mopping the floor, shopping and cooking, cleaning, and scrubbing along with the other household chores. She continued managing these duties while caring for our family when my father returned to work four years later.

My step-grandmother never gave me what she gave to her other grand-kids. To her, I was the cursed child, and she continued saying this even when I finished medical school. During my medical studies, I remember her saying that my parents were wasting money on me, as nobody would marry me.

However, my mother never talked back to her. If she wanted to say anything, she would say it to my father. In front of her mother-in-law, she remained a submissive lady other than when she spoke up for me.

As my physiotherapy progressed, I began to regain some muscle strength. The first area to improve was my arms; they became almost completely normal. My left leg also improved. My right leg was the most affected because it had zero muscle power. Even now, my quadricep (knee extensor) still has zero muscle power. My hamstring (knee flexor) likewise has zero muscle power. My buttock, the gluteal region where I sit, has not recovered, although it has plus-two power. It did improve for a time, but with age, I've returned to the same level as before. The best outcome is walking without aid, though I still wear the same brace. I am grateful.

Education was important in our family. During the first four years of my illness, my mother was not confident of my recovery. She was not sure I would start walking even with a brace. Concerned the public schools might not accept me, she began educating herself so she could homeschool me if necessary. By age seven, a certain amount of strength and power returned to my body, and my mother grew confident that I would someday complete my studies and become a doctor.

Initially, the medical team said I would need a brace for all four limbs - four braces. But it would depend on the amount of effort that was exerted. With continuous day and night exercise, my arms completely improved. Both parents took turns helping me exercise in those four years when my father was home. That is one of the reasons my body regained some power. As my arms grew stronger, my mother felt hopeful that my recovery would continue.

"Your arms are so much better now," she smiled one evening while massaging them. "I am confident we can help you continue to improve. I'll make you a doctor in a field that is toughest for women – cardiology!"

That's when she asked some of the neighbors to give us children's books. In our region, school starts from class one, and it goes up to tenth grade. Eleventh and twelfth grades are completed in college.

Mom asked for books so she could teach herself to read and help me learn, too. She used picture books to divert my attention from constantly looking at my arms and legs. With polio, the feet get deformed because of dwindling strength and ability as well as the gravity effect. I would study my feet and look for changes that might signal atrophy.

Mom received several first-grade books, and my parents began reading them to me.

"Look, my child," my mother said one day. "I'm studying with you." She held up a book and read the page to me. She slowly and gradually continued studying the ABCs, mathematics, and other important school subjects to prepare herself to teach if needed.

At the onset of the diagnosis, our family was plunged into what we called the Dark Age as we struggled with disappointment and discouragement. But with progressive improvement in my condition, life and cheer returned to our home. We were not rich. We were not even middle class. We were lower middle class. We didn't have a television, but we tried to entertain ourselves the best way we could. Sometimes we played word games or invented stories. Relatives and friends came to visit.

I studied at home, beginning at age five, because I was intelligent. My mother and father taught me the basics like English, mathematics, and regional subjects as well as our local language. Learning new things was exciting, so I mastered the subjects quickly.

When my father eventually resumed his job, he took a position lower than what he had before because of the four-year unemployment gap. Whatever the job entailed, he accepted it because we needed money at home. There were many expenses because of my health, including the physiotherapist fees. In addition, my siblings attended public school, and they needed money for books and transportation.

As I continued learning at home, my mind moved quickly! I'm so grateful that even if God took something from me, he gave me so much, including a good mind. Family and friends know me as the lady with three brains!

I used to give my parents advice, but sometimes they didn't understand. Occasionally, I felt like people in Pakistan were unenlightened. Some would say the white people were intelligent, but they didn't understand, either. Whenever the things I predicted would materialize, I said, "Look, I told you this would happen. You did not grasp it. If you develop this kind of program, for example, this may not work." I did calculations to show the objective was not achievable. Then I realized the problem was not with my family or coworkers; the problem was with me. My mind is strong, and I'm gifted mentally. I can predict certain outcomes and think ahead, and I continue to develop mentally with education. Not that I have a special talent, but my brain is sharp. Even after marriage, sometimes I would get upset with my husband and say, "Don't you get what I'm talking about?" I would think ahead and expect him, and everyone around me, to keep up.

Initially, the medical experts wanted my father to put me in a special school. But there was no concept of special schools in our area. Some family members, including my step-grandmother, urged my parents to abandon me and place me in an orphanage, arguing that as I grew older, no one would marry me. But my parents didn't listen, knowing that our family was far more committed to my care and well-being than an orphanage or school would be. My father wanted to make sure that I was educated in a public school when he and my mother had taught me all they could, so he enrolled me at the age of six in a girls' school. He would drop me off in the morning. In the afternoon, a servant would pick me up. Our house was not far, half a mile or so. My brother took a horse ride to school (his school was close to mine), and I was so jealous. I cried and screamed that I wanted to take a horse ride as well, but my father said no.

"Evaluate her," he urged the administrators and teachers. "She's had a solid start at home, and she's ready to learn more."

So they evaluated me. The first year I only studied a month or so and passed all my subjects. The school let me skip grade one and promoted me to grade two. Because of my self-confidence in learning, I felt I could study lightly and play around.

My classroom teacher and homeroom teacher were strictly advised not to let me do any of that. They instructed me to stay focused on my studies instead of taking recess with the other children. My father paid extra for the staff to supervise added homework. Sometimes I felt deprived of playtime. Later, I understood why. My family and the teachers feared that if I played outside with the other children, I might fall and get hurt. For the first six to eight years of my education, I did not play with the other students when there was a break. I never went outside. I stayed in the classroom with either the teacher or a security guard. We didn't have a cafeteria; none of the schools did. Students brought their lunches. I used to eat in class and work on lessons while the other students played outside. Classes ran from eight a.m. to one p.m., and I would be in the classroom the entire time.

So, that's how life was initially. I was fully focused on my studies. If there were any social events, someone stayed home with me. I didn't go anywhere to socialize. This was a protective gesture since my condition was more like a taboo and people would make mean remarks about me, hurting my mom and dad. I was not aware of this until I reached sixth or seventh grade.

After sixth grade, my father allowed me to go outside during break time, and that was a wonderful opportunity to make new friends: Fatima, Nuzhat, Irshad, and Loveta. I started enjoying life more, even though my main goal was to study. Sadly, after leaving school, I got disconnected from my school friends for over forty years. But recently I did find Fatima, Nuzhat, and Irshad through another friend, Christine. Christine's family rented Fatima's house in Karachi, and Fatima introduced me to Christine. Christine is much older than me, and to this day, she is my best friend. Christine moved to the U.S. in 1991, while I was in medical school in Pakistan. However, I stayed in touch with Christine. She recently connected me with Fatima, who connected me with Nuzhat and Irshad. Fatima also connected me with one of my favorite school teachers, Ms. Zehra, who is now eighty years old. We still talk about school days and relive wonderful memories.

Sunita Dodani receiving school degree

I finished those twelve years of education in ten years because I took double classes since I was quick to study and learn, always earning A grades.

My illness also impacted our parents' social habits. My father had been more of an extrovert at his job. My mom was very sociable. But after my diagnosis, with criticism from the family and no support from the in-laws, she became aloof. Although she had a type A personality, she didn't get stressed quickly, and she avoided going out in public. When I was eleven or twelve, my father took me out for the first time to the market.

That day, I could see that people around us were laughing at me and making comments that I could hear. The second time, he took me to a different market just for vegetable shopping. At first, I didn't say anything. Then as I was looking around and listening to the shoppers' cruel comments, I said, "Let's go," being my usual

15

authoritative self. I said again, "Dad, let's go home. I'm not enjoying this." Days later, it happened for the third time.

When he wanted to take me out in public again, I said, "Don't you see the problem? Are you not reading your daughter? People are mocking me. They are imitating my walk. This is hurtful."

My father kept telling me each time that people would not change. "They will remain what they are. You must change yourself. You must put your mind above their minds. Then these things will not hurt you." I didn't understand then, but I do now.

I stopped going to the market for some time. But then my mother said, "It is you who's going to suffer." My father added, "If you don't go to the market and meet the public, you will become socially isolated."

By then I slowly understood what they meant was that it was me who had to change. If you think the entire world will sympathize with you, the world will sympathize with you. But I don't need sympathy. I need encouragement. My parents wanted to make me strong - emotionally and mentally strong.

After finishing tenth grade in 1985, I had surgery on my right foot before joining St. Joseph College for eleventh and twelfth grades. In Pakistan and many developing countries, we have just two years of undergraduate college whereas the U.S. has four-year college programs. I attended a girls' college, and then I enrolled in medical school in a co-education program. This was a culture shock, but we will get into that later.

Chapter Three

My Path to Becoming a Doctor

I finished my regular education through tenth grade at age fourteen, which was early. My parents and I began to consider the next steps in my education to prepare me for a professional career. My right leg, which had been affected by polio, had improved with exercise, a full leg brace, and mobility over time. However, we consulted the doctor to see if anything else could be done to enhance joint flexibility and reduce falls. I could walk with bare feet but with an abnormal gait and an inverted right foot. Even with the brace, I fell quite often.

The orthopedic surgeon recommended surgery on my right foot to bring it into a neutral position (straight). He believed the procedure would fix the ankle joint and facilitate the use of my polio-affected foot to move more comfortably and remain stable. He would fuse the ankle joint, a procedure called triple arthrodesis (fusion of three joints of the hindfoot and midfoot, the subtalar joint) to stop the falls.

The surgery was successful. I stayed in the hospital for a month, and my brother Roop, who is two years older than me, stayed with me the entire time. During my recovery, I grew closer to Roop. He and I would share family memories, and he would tell me what was happening at our school and among our friends. I will always remain indebted to my brother for his unwavering support throughout my life. During my hospital stay, he not only assisted with my recovery but also took care of my personal needs, ensuring I was comfortable and well-cared for. Roop and I finished schooling around the same time, even though I was younger because I doubled my course load and took two classes simultaneously. Roop and I had the same classes and assignments, so we helped each other.

Hospitals sometimes don't care much about a patient's emotional needs, but children do better with family support. After surgery, I became close to all my siblings; however, my closeness with Roop and my sister Sarla was more than with the others. Roop was the first in the family who pursue higher education in the U.S. after graduating from high school in Karachi, Pakistan. He secretly applied to several universities in the U.S. and one day announced he had passed the Test of English as a Foreign Language (TOEFL) and had been accepted for undergraduate study at Iowa State University in Des Moines, Iowa. My father was only able to furnish a one-semester fee for him, and the rest my brother earned through college jobs and scholarships. Although we all missed him, everyone was happy that Roop had this exciting opportunity to study abroad. I would become the second to leave Pakistan for the U.S., but more about that later.

The foot surgery reduced my falls, although it took almost three months to complete my full recovery. Another issue was the living style in Pakistan, which is not made for people with special needs. The concept of accessible homes and bathrooms did not exist there until recently. For example, toilets in most developing countries are built into the floor – not like the common American seat toilet. My father had switched to the Western commode style during our college years because it was hard for me to squat and use the Asian type. Our home was on the third floor of the building, and I went up and down the steps several times daily. An advantage to that was I gained more muscle power from enhanced mobility and step climbing. My right leg muscle power improved from 0 power to 1 power, and in some muscles, it was 2.

Slowly I recovered from surgery and was ready to get admitted to St. Joseph College for the eleventh and twelfth grades. Attending an all-girls institution provided a comfortable environment where I could confidently display my strong leadership and authoritative manner. I formed many friendships and enthusiastically participated in extracurricular activities, including outdoor picnics, carnivals, fairs, and zoo visits. The foot surgery I had undergone bolstered my confidence and instilled a newfound sense of stability. Choosing the Pre-Medicine track with the ambition of attending medical school, I found immense support from my teachers, who were always understanding and sympathetic. As usual, I maintained my status as a high achiever and honors student. This phase of my life felt like a journey of rediscovering the strengths I had lost after contracting polio. I paid little mind to the comments or remarks about my abnormal gait, focusing instead on attending family gatherings such as weddings and ladies' parties with newfound confidence. I held onto my father's wise words: "The world will not change; it is you who must change and rise above the remarks of others, ensuring they do not hurt you."

About this time, my family and I began discussing my future in earnest. My mother had always wanted me to become a doctor. In Pakistan, you can matriculate immediately into college and medical school after your twelve-year education. My passion, however, was to become a fashion model or businesswoman. While my journey at the Aga Khan University (AKU) is detailed in Chapter Four, I do want to mention here that the chair of the AKU selection committee, Dr. Rukhsana Zuberi, was also the Associate Dean for medical education and later became my supervisor of the Family Medicine residency program. Many years later, she told me that at the time of the interviews, there was a bit of hesitancy in providing AKU medical school admission. I was a high scorer in the SAT and TOEFL examinations, and all interviews were exceptional, although a single concern was raised. Medical school requires long schedules, some at night, and traveling to outlying communities – would that exhaust me? Could I do it?

Dr. Zuberi told me that she was the one who voted for me and very strongly told the selection committee, "Yes, she should be able to do those things. I see a very bright future in her." The discussions were to safeguard me, and she put her foot down and said, "We need people like her." I will always remain grateful to Dr. Zuberi for her support and confidence.

Last week, I found myself in the hot seat, interviewed by a U.S. media channel about my life journey and the successes I've achieved despite battling polio most of my life. The anchor hit me with this question: "Along this journey of 52 years with polio – what do you still feel perplexed about? For what do you still have no answers?"

It sent my mind spinning into the past, searching for answers to two enduring mysteries. Ever since my diagnosis with polio and my father's return to his government job, I couldn't help but notice his meticulous approach to our family's affairs and business matters. His penchant for organization left an indelible mark on me; I learned the importance of orderliness from him. He was adamant about filing away every document, refusing to discard even the smallest piece of paper. From the moment polio entered our lives until his passing in 2017, he maintained a file dedicated solely to my polio-related health. This file, dating back to 1972, cataloged every aspect of my journey with polio: from diagnosis to surgeries, rehabilitation to consultations with orthopedic surgeons. He carried this file with him everywhere, even into his final days, burdened by persistent guilt and a sense of responsibility for my condition.

Despite his tireless efforts to seek out new therapies and specialists, he never forgave himself for not ensuring I received the three drops of vaccine that could have spared me from polio. He held onto the hope that I would one day lead a "normal" life, even as I recovered, married, welcomed a child, and found professional success. The question of why he made that choice still haunts me to this day.

The other perplexing question that lingers in my mind is how people respond to me, both those who know me and those who don't. I often question whether their kindness and praise stem from genuine admiration for my accomplishments despite my limitations, or if it's merely born out of pity. This is a conundrum that continues to puzzle me, even as I navigate life's challenges and triumphs.

CHAPTER FOUR

The Road to Cardiology: Training and Research Adventures

My education through the twelfth grade took place at girls' schools and colleges. In Karachi, Pakistan, the education system consists of schooling from grades one through ten, after which grades eleven and twelve are attended at colleges. As mentioned in Chapter Three, I completed my schooling up to the tenth grade at Jesus and Mary School. I then advanced to St. Joseph College, where I finished grades eleven and twelve, specializing in Pre-Medicine.

After finishing twelfth grade at St. Joseph College, I found myself with a nine- to ten-month break before the start of medical school. My mother, who was highly intelligent and ambitious for my future, had always wanted me to become a doctor, and I was eager to pursue this path to make her happy. However, she also believed in preparing me for all eventualities. During this break, she ensured I acquired additional skills to become self-sufficient in case I didn't end up practicing medicine. First, she enrolled me in a culinary school, where I developed a passion for cooking and learned a wide range of culinary techniques. Simultaneously, she enrolled me in stitching and knitting classes in a special school, skills I also came to enjoy. Cooking, however, became my passion. I participated in numerous cooking contests in Karachi and consistently won at both local and national levels. I even had the opportunity to teach cooking at a hotel in Pakistan. Despite my family's doubts about my potential to become a doctor, my mother never wavered in her belief in me. In hindsight, her insistence on diversifying my skills was invaluable.

To this day, I enjoy cooking immensely and often muse that if I weren't a cardiologist, I could have been a successful chef, earning more than I do now.

Applying for medical school was quite a journey. Many public medical schools in the country have some level of political involvement, which frequently disrupts the academic schedule. Although the official duration of medical education in Pakistan is five years after twelfth grade, most students end up taking six or seven years to graduate due to interruptions caused by political rallies and interference in the educational process. My parents wanted to give me the best, and at the same time, also wanted to make sure that I was on a speedy pathway for medical school training.

Fortunately, around the time I was applying, some excellent private medical schools emerged. Aga Khan University (AKU) stands out as one of the finest institutions in Pakistan. It is a prestigious institution renowned for its commitment to academic excellence and health care. Founded in 1983 by His Highness the Aga Khan, AKU has developed into a leading university that combines rigorous academic programs with a strong emphasis on community service and research. The university offers a wide range of undergraduate, graduate, and professional courses primarily focusing on health sciences, including a renowned Medical College and School of Nursing and Midwifery. AKU's campus in Karachi is equipped with state-of-the-art facilities, including the Aga Khan University Hospital, which serves as both a teaching hospital and a premier healthcare institution providing high-quality medical care to the community. The university is also dedicated to advancing knowledge through research, with numerous initiatives and collaborations aimed at addressing critical health and social issues in Pakistan and beyond. In addition to its academic and healthcare contributions, AKU emphasizes holistic development, encouraging students to engage in extracurricular activities and community outreach. This comprehensive approach ensures that AKU graduates are well-prepared to meet the challenges of their profession and make meaningful contributions to society. AKU's impact extends globally, with campuses and programs in several countries.

Being accepted into AKU was incredibly challenging. Applicants first had to pass the Scholastic Assessment Test (SAT) and Test of English as a Foreign Language (TOEFL) examinations. Only those with the highest scores were invited to proceed to a series of interviews. I was truly fortunate to be among the 100 students selected for admission from over 5000 applicants in 1987. This rigorous selection process made my acceptance feel like a significant achievement and a crucial step toward my medical career. Getting accepted into AKU was a dream come true. Years of family support despite financial limitations and extended relatives' criticism had bolstered my confidence, so a medical degree became a realistic goal. Having learned to deal with the physical and emotional struggles of polio for the first sixteen years of my life, I was encouraged to hope that I might one day become a physician to help others with similar problems.

My father was the only breadwinner for our family, working a modestly paid government job. Given the high tuition fees at AKU, I was fortunate to receive financial aid that allowed me to complete medical school within five years. While I was happy to be admitted to AKU, this was my first experience in a co-educational setting, studying alongside both male and female students. My past experiences with the public, where I was often laughed at and shamed, made me apprehensive about how my new classmates would treat me because of my polio. I was scared and a bit skeptical about how the boys would react. However, as you will read below, my classmates proved my fears were unfounded, as both the boys and girls showered me with support and kindness. Their encouragement played a crucial role in my success, allowing me to thrive in this new, inclusive environment.

I was among the top scorers in the AKU entrance examinations (SAT and TOEFL) and received glowing remarks during the interviews. However, my first year of medical school was fraught with unexpected obstacles and challenges. I had previously been enrolled in female-only classrooms. At AKU, there was a slightly higher number of boys than girls in my classes, about sixty percent boys and forty percent girls. I felt awkward in this unfamiliar environment. Despite having a very vocal personality, in my first year at AKU, I hesitated to speak up and draw unwanted attention since the male relatives in our extended family had been known to criticize my existence and my parents' willingness to send me to medical school. They felt, as did many in the public population, that sons were more deserving of parent-sponsored education than daughters were. I had been viewed as a hindrance or even a drain on our family's and society's resources. I assumed the boys in my first year of medical school would feel the same disdain.

I kept quiet and seldom volunteered answers to the professor's questions in class. In small group activities, I let the others do the talking. If I were to contribute to the discussion, I worried that I would be ridiculed or discredited. Concern over the noticeable effects of polio on my body and possible public reactions kept me quiet and subdued in an academic environment that was otherwise intellectually stimulating. This was not the personality I was born with, but I forced myself to remain quiet.

To make the situation worse, I began experiencing new bodily symptoms that were uncomfortable as well as embarrassing. The ongoing stress of adjusting to the unfamiliar environment at AKU led to some gastrointestinal (GI) health issues, including stomach pain and intestinal incontinence, with frequent bathroom trips during classes. Many times when flare-ups occurred, I found it impossible to wait long hours and often had to excuse myself from the classroom, feeling the weight of every questioning eye. While people with normal legs could reach the bathroom in time, my slower gait due to polio meant I had to hurry to avoid accidents, which added to my anxiety and embarrassment. Sometimes the fierce pressure would not result in a bowel movement, but I could not afford to "wait and see."

My health condition worsened, and I noticed blood mixed with stool. I told my mother. She said, "It's due to stress or periods, or it's just an upset stomach."

"No, Mom," I replied. "I know the difference between a period and these episodes."

I could not discuss my symptoms with anyone in my class of 100 students, as I knew no one beforehand. Although some of the girls in my small groups were friendly, I tended to remain aloof, trying to cope with these personal challenges on my own. I didn't tell anyone else and certainly not my classmates, fearing ostracism, humiliation, or rejection as well as university expulsion if the administration found out!

Fortunately, my older sister was in her third year of medical study at a public medical university. She recommended a doctor who prescribed an anti-motility drug, Lomotil, a medication used for diarrhea symptoms. I started taking Lomotil when I was under stress due to anxieties like an upcoming exam, for example. The medicine would work for eight to ten hours.

The five years of medical education at AKU included mandatory Community Health Services (CHS) rotations. These rotations involved weekly visits to low-income communities to understand residents' needs and provide health care services as part of our training. Each week, we spent many hours in these communities, visiting households to understand the social determinants of health and to build rapport with families. Each student group was assigned to a specific community to become familiar with the local population's health issues. The bus trips to reach these areas lasted about forty minutes and brought us to a small community center with a tiny bathroom, which was agony for someone with bowel issues. To manage my condition, I took Lomotil daily to prevent frequent restroom trips. However, when we were in the community, I avoided eating or drinking anything due to my fear of needing a restroom. The bathrooms at AKU community clinics were inconvenient for me, as they had low toilet seats and lacked accessible facilities. The concept of appropriate facilities for people with special needs is nonexistent in Pakistan. Many villagers who were our patients lived in mud huts that were accessed by climbing small hills. I didn't think I could make it, but my classmates insisted on helping me in reaching the homes assigned to my group.

The first two years were particularly nightmarish. I struggled in my studies, and my scores in annual exams began falling. Many times during exams I had to excuse myself and rush to the restroom. Despite these challenges, none of my classmates, not even my closest friends, knew what I was enduring during those years at AKU. I kept my struggles private, persevering through the difficulties alone.

My health condition eventually began deteriorating as I was losing weight, unable to eat much food, and experiencing worsening GI symptoms. My sister and father took me to a gastroenterologist outside of AKU as I was scared that if I revealed my health at AKU, I would be expelled. The doctor put me on huge doses of steroids, and my symptoms would subside for a time. Eventually, however, the medicine lost its effectiveness. I developed the common side effects of steroids (weight gain, central obesity, and a puffy face). Doctor shopping continued as my symptoms did not consistently improve. Another doctor diagnosed an infection and prescribed antibiotics, which didn't help for long. I was coping but miserable. I became depressed and frustrated, which often manifested in my attitude as expressed to my parents:

"You should've listened to my grandparents! Why didn't you put me in an orphanage?" I complained to them. "Other families don't put up with health problems like polio. Now I have another medical issue to deal with." Thankfully, my parents and siblings helped me through this period of doubt. However, complications arose.

I struggled through my studies, but I became more self-conscious about my health and physical presence than ever. I had been rejected by men in my family – uncles, and cousins – as well as by the general population, especially men who viewed me as inferior and fit only for domestic work at home. To avoid male rejection at college, I refused to draw attention to myself and kept my head down as much as possible. In the first year, after classes, I would go alone to the library basement to study.

The boys in my class and my student group were friendly. It was me who felt insecure among them. One of my classmates, Omar Darr, noticed I was not mixing with the rest, so he would do silly things to make our group giggle. Jokingly, he would make funny comments to get a response from me and bring a laugh. Similarly, other boys - Muneer, Naresh, Bilal, JP, Imran, Shehryar, and more - tried to make me feel comfortable. I started making friends and getting involved in small group discussions that involved boys and girls.

My good friends Azima, Mubina, Saira, Samina, Saba, Humaira, Lubna from AKU pharmacy, and many more were exceedingly kind. It's been over 34 years since we graduated from AKU, but all those classmates are now close friends, and we would do anything for each other. Particularly, Saira is remarkably close to me, and we visit each other often. Saira was also my roommate in a girls' hostel, when we completed electives in Lahore, Pakistan, in the final year of the medical program. Although I lost touch with Omar after graduating from medical school, we resumed contact when he became a cardiac surgeon at Yale University, which overlaps with my cardiology specialization.

As the years progressed, I relaxed and became more comfortable studying with boys in class and in our discussion groups. The academic pressure was strong with both a British and an American education system in place. Reading was intense and demanding. We were all plunging through our medical studies together, and the boys, far from remaining aloof, just wanted to be friends with us girls as fellow students.

Despite these adjustments, my studies did not improve because of failing GI health. By my second year of medical studies, I still could not cope with coursework. I lost 30 to 40 pounds. All students were assigned academic advisers. My adviser was Dr. Shoro, the Head of Anatomy and a nice person (God rest his soul in peace). During the first year, we had regular meetings and discussed my failing grades. He was concerned, but I never shared with him all that I was going through.

One day, he called me in his office: "You must tell me what's bothering you. You were an honors student with top grades. What has happened to disrupt your studies? You look unwell. I noticed you have been leaving the classroom frequently, and I followed you once to see where you were going, which of course was the restroom. A thought came to mind that you are cheating and going to the lavatory to look for exam answers. But I noticed you leave in the middle of regular classes also, so it was not just during exams." The concern in his eyes was genuine. I was scared to tell him but knew I had to.

"Dr. Shoro, soon after joining AKU, I began having abnormal gut issues, and I'm trying to get a proper diagnosis for my symptoms."

"I'm concerned about your academic progress," he said kindly. "I have checked your previous exams, and one thing that has stood out is that you are doing poorly in classes and exams not because you don't know, but because you are not completing the assignments and not answering all questions." He explained, "In all exams, you have completed one-third or at most half the exam with correct answers. Further, your responses are accurate and professionally written, but all questions are not attempted."

When Dr. Shoro said that, I felt comfortable that a well-wisher had been keeping a close eye on me. As discreetly as possible, I described my symptoms, and he referred me to a gastroenterologist within AKU, Dr. Wasim Jafri, to whom I will remain indebted for the rest of my life.

Dr. Jafri scheduled a colonoscopy for me. A colonoscopy is a diagnostic procedure by which gastroenterologists view the gut (colon) and make diagnoses based on the gut structure and biopsies. My test led to a diagnosis of ulcerative colitis (ulcers in the colon with inflammation), which is an autoimmune disease that affects more women than men. At the end of the colonoscopy, Dr. Jafri said, "Sunita, I wish you would have come to me earlier. Had you come soon after noticing symptoms, you would have just a small portion of your colon involved. Currently, your whole colon (gut) is red and inflamed, but we will treat it."

I told him that I had visited many doctors, but alas, they had misdiagnosed me and given me the wrong treatments. I later told him I was afraid that I would be expelled as AKU could pronounce me as an unsuitable candidate for medical education!

I began educating myself on this condition to learn all I could and explore any association of ulcerative colitis with polio. Of course, there was none as polio is caused by infection, and ulcerative colitis is an autoimmune disease, meaning the cause is unknown. Originating in the intestines, it can cause joint pain and affect any bodily organ. Dr. Jafri took diligent care of me with the right treatment. My symptoms improved gradually. However, the first three years at AKU were a nightmare in this regard.

I continued studying ulcerative colitis after realizing I had to take care of myself even more, having both polio and autoimmune disease. I was depressed that now, in addition to polio, I have to deal with an autoimmune disease too, for which there is no cure. Flare-ups in the condition could occur at any time but were mostly caused by stress. As I learned about common triggers, I understood the symptoms had become severe due to the stress of medical education. One flare-up led to an overnight hospital stay for a blood transfusion. Nobody from my class knew what I was going through, and nobody knew to date.

Dr. Jafri monitored my symptoms and general health. He put me on huge doses of steroids – oral prednisone – which helped. Fortunately, I did not have to take the stronger medications that could cause serious side effects, for which I'm thankful.

During my university days, I lived a double life. At home, I was loved by my family. Leaving the house at seven a.m., I would encounter public contempt until I reached the university forty minutes later. In the halls of higher education, I was accepted and supported by well-meaning professors and kind classmates who treated me as an equal. As my health stabilized after the transfusion and while taking medication, my former childhood confidence revived. Slowly, I developed a leadership role in the class, especially among the boys. They started to see me as a strong and capable female fighter!

Never would I have expected this. Not only had I been shy and reserved when beginning my medical education, but I was also acutely aware of the different treatment experienced by females. To date, girls in Pakistan are considered second-class citizens, raised to become wives and mothers while tending to homes and caring for husbands. Females often receive a partial or inferior education compared to boys, with limited career opportunities. My family had nurtured my academic and professional goals and encouraged my social development. Although my parents began urging me to attend social events like weddings and graduations, I usually declined, unwilling to be mocked or ignored, having suffered too many insults for years. However, this was not the case at our house, where both my sister and I were treated equally or even better than my brothers.

In the third year of my medical education, as my confidence grew, my strong personality again emerged. I was ready to speak my mind for what was right and give female students equal opportunities with male students. I even slapped a boy who said dreadful things about the girls! Our female classmates learned to trust my assertiveness and willingness to represent them.

During the fourth and fifth years of medical school, we were enrolled in clinical rotations at AKU Hospital. These involved twelve to sixteen hours of night shifts that could be intense. I did considerable walking through the wards, up and down the halls, and taking the stairs. My weaker leg became stronger. If I felt overwhelmed or if my ulcerative colitis flared up, I would take steroids to calm things down. In Pakistan, medicines, including cancer drugs, are readily available at the pharmacy without a prescription.

Sunita Dodani with AKU classmates in Lahore, Pakistan

For the final year of my medical program, our group, which consisted of seven boys and six girls, went to Lahore, Pakistan, and stayed in a hostel. I was the leader of the group and dictated the agenda to everyone. My parents knew all my friends as most visited our home. My father particularly trusted Shehryar, and after one visit, he told him,

"Son, take care of Sunita."

"Uncle, she takes care of us," said Shehryar laughingly.

Lahore offered an exciting new vista of medical study, and I completed several electives during the fifth year of medical school. Throughout my journey, my parents continued to support me wholeheartedly. As graduation approached, my father was determined to ensure that I could become independent by learning to drive. Due to my right leg polio condition, I needed a special automatic car with a left-side gas pedal using my unaffected leg. However, importing custom-free automatic cars into Pakistan was banned because of past abuses of this privilege.

Sunita Dodani at AKU graduation dinner handing automatic car request letter to a government official

For our graduation dinner, AKU invited several Pakistani government officials. Seizing the opportunity, my father wrote a letter requesting permission to import a custom-free automatic car from Japan. I handed his letter to a government official at the event. Remarkably, within six months, I received a permit to import a custom-free automatic car with a left-side gas pedal. This was a significant step toward independence, made possible by my parents' unwavering support!

Dodani received a Medical Degree from AKU in 1992

I received my medical degree, called an MBBS (MD), following five years of training. Extending my education, I completed a year-long internship at AKU followed by three years of Family Medicine residency, a postgraduate training (1993-1996) with a concentration in preventive cardiology. Though I also passed both Step 1 and Step 2 of the U.S. Medical Licensing Examination (USMLE), I decided to pursue postgraduate training in Pakistan to fulfill my mother's dream to show the Pakistani public what I can do despite polio. During my internship, I rotated through several disciplines, including emergency medicine, where 12-hour shifts required full attention without sleep. Sometimes I did double shifts for 24 hours. Even though I often felt physically tired, I loved my job.

Around 1994, while completing my residency, I received a duty-free automatic car imported from Japan, which increased my independence. I learned to drive with the help of my driver, and after passing the driving exam, I began taking the car. As my residency often required late hours, I frequently drove myself to AKU, enjoying the newfound freedom and convenience.

My three years of residency were interesting. The first year included three-month rotations in major medical disciplines: medicine, surgery, obstetrics and gynecology, and community health services. The second year focused on subspecialties such as pulmonology, critical care, cardiothoracic surgery, and additional cardiology.

The training program coordinators, Drs. Philip Johnson and Gregory Raglow were from the U.S. Dr. Johnson started the residency program in 1993, and Dr. Raglow joined him in 1995. I was among the first batch of five residents in the Family Medicine residency program at AKU. This was tough but exceptional training.

Sunita Dodani with Dr. Gregory Raglow

Sunita Dodani with Dr. Philip Johnson

It was during the second year of my residency that I developed a strong interest in cardiology while working with Dr. Khawar Kazmi, the head of cardiology. Dr. Kazmi was exceedingly kind and a thorough cardiologist. I would stay after completing my day with him to learn more about EKGs, echocardiograms, and angiographies.

In the third year of study, we had a mandatory six-month rotation: three months in the remote northern part of Pakistan, in the city of Singal, and the remaining three months at a Christian charity hospital in Abbottabad, Punjab. I went to both places alone and completed my six-month elective.

At Singal, a mountainous area, we first traveled by helicopter. After that, we endured a six-hour drive along a narrow, winding, and treacherous road. There was an Aga Khan Hospital in Singal, Pakistan, where we stayed and served the rural communities. For three months, I ate the same regional food and stayed in a small room with an attached bathroom. Thankfully, the bathroom had a toilet seat. I very much enjoyed working at Singal Hospital, performing surgeries, and seeing patients.

Similarly, my elective at the Christian Bach Hospital in Abbottabad was an amazing experience. Collaborating with missionaries was a delight. I stayed with a nurse, Debbie, in her house, which was within the hospital compound. Debbie was friendly and helpful. The hospital surgeon, Dr. Luke, and his wife Nancy had come from the U.S. and had been serving there for over 30 years. Even today, I am in touch with Dr. Luke and Nancy from whom I learned so much.

Sunita Dodani's electives during residency training in Abbottabad, Pakistan

Working at Bach involved seeing patients, both in clinics as well as admitted patients, assisting with surgeries, and participating in on-call rotations that sometimes lasted up to 36 hours. Toward the end of my rotation, my father and sister visited me in Abbottabad. We enjoyed family time, went horseback riding, and had a great deal of fun.

While many classmates left Pakistan after graduation to pursue further studies abroad, particularly in the U.S., I chose to stay. I wanted to fulfill my mother's dream of proving to our community that, as she had promised, I could become a doctor and care for not only my family but also thousands of others. Those relatives who had once doubted me, saying I would have a useless life, now express admiration. My uncles and aunts, formerly skeptical, now say they wish their children could be like me. This transformation in perspective is a testament to the journey and accomplishments that have defined my life while navigating a series of challenging circumstances.

Chapter Five

Professional Heights but Personal Hurdles:
Quest for a Soulmate

After completing my medical residency (postgraduate training) from 1993 to 1996, I accepted a faculty position in the Department of Family Medicine at AKU in October 1996 with a joint appointment in the Division of Cardiology and the Department of Internal Medicine in 1998. This was an exciting opportunity to experience an instructional role in the medical field. It was great to share the training I received during my studies and help new medical students find their way through the program.

During the 1997-98 academic year, I received further postgraduate-level training in preventive cardiology, also known as a fellowship. This path initially stemmed from my mother's dream for me to enter a challenging field for women, with cardiology being one of the toughest, alongside surgery. As mentioned earlier, my interest in cardiology developed during my fourth-year rotation in the cardiology division. Dr. Kazmi, the head of cardiology and later my mentor, recognized my potential. A visionary leader, he was a strong advocate for increasing women's presence in cardiology.

During those two years of training, I immersed myself not only in clinical practice but also in research. This dual focus provided me with additional time and experience, significantly enhancing my preparation for a career in this field. I dedicated 16 to 18 hours each day at the hospital, eager to learn as much as possible from Dr. Kazmi. My training involved extensive hours in the cardiac catheterization lab (Cath Lab), where I observed and later assisted with angiographies, interpreted EKGs and echocardiograms, took extra shifts in the emergency department to manage cardiology patient admissions, and co-authored numerous manuscripts for publication with Dr. Kazmi. These two years in preventive cardiology solidified my reputation as a hardworking physician. As a testament to his trust and confidence, Dr. Kazmi assigned me to run my clinic with minimal supervision. I cherish his trust to this day. In 1998, I made my first visit to the U.S. with my mother to see my brother and explore some elective opportunities in cardiology for my medical training. By then, my brother Roop, who has always been incredibly supportive, had completed his undergraduate degree at the University of Iowa Des Moines, Iowa, and a master's degree in computer science from the Colorado State University in Fort Collins, Colorado. From there he relocated to Boulder, Colorado, and was hired at Oracle, an international database management company.

Sunita Dodani with her mother on first visit to the United States in 1998

This trip was exhilarating, and my mother and I enjoyed it to the fullest. We landed at the John F. Kennedy Airport in New York, and the first thing I noticed was that no one was staring at me! Was something wrong with these travelers and airport employees? Not a single person was giving me "that look"! Instead, people gave us a nice smile and said "hello." It was a pleasant surprise. Unfortunately, in our culture, it is not customary to greet strangers at all, much less with a warm smile. Maybe this was just an airport thing? The first thought that came to mind was This is the world where I would be best suited; I want to leave Pakistan.

The next day, according to our plan, we went to see the Statue of Liberty and the Twin Towers. Moving around in the busy city without strangers gawking at me was a profound change from what I was used to in Pakistan.

"Look, Mom, they're not staring at me – they just smile like they do for everyone."

My mother was happy to see this distinct shift in public perception from our previous experience. I was on top of the world to have that feeling that nobody noticed how I walked or how I looked. We also drove to Boston to meet one of my father's college friends, Uncle Tikam.

We had such a fun time!

After the first week, we went to Boulder, Colorado, and stayed with my brother for another week. Before arrival, I had already established contact with the University of Colorado College of Medicine in Denver with Dr. Calvin Wilson. Roop drove me to Denver and again, to my surprise, I was greeted with joy and delight. Dr. Wilson wanted me to come and collaborate with him and complete some electives, to which I agreed. This was a different world!

In 1999, I returned to Boulder, Colorado, to complete two months of training with Dr. Wilson. Every morning, Roop would drop me off at the bus stop, where I would catch a bus that took me straight to the university campus in Denver. The commute took an hour (one way), but it was worth it for the experience. Those two months with my brother brought us even closer. Since he was not married then, we had plenty of time to spend together after work. We took short weekend trips to explore Colorado and enjoyed some exciting excursions. The American junk food like McDonald's, Burger King, and others was delightful as we did not have these fast-food options in Pakistan. Every Friday night was McDonald's night with a large fries bucket.

The university campus was great, and everyone I met was incredibly nice, making my time there even more enjoyable. Following that period, I frequently traveled to the U.S. and Canada to make presentations at scientific meetings and conferences. These international engagements enabled me to build valuable connections, highlight my skills and capabilities, and explore opportunities to work in the U.S. Sometimes, I traveled as often as weekly to the U.S., which normally is a 32- to 36-hour trip (one-way). Despite the exhaustion, I enjoyed the travel and felt invigorated by the academic experiences.

My career was progressing, and my leadership and clinical skills were increasingly recognized at AKU. I became the preferred physician cardiologist for most of the faculty and staff. Most celebrities preferred to see me. My clinical acumen was honed through the excellent training I received from the outstanding instructors at AKU and further enhanced by additional training at the University of Colorado, Denver, which was truly remarkable. In 2000, driven by my interest in research, I conducted Pakistan's first national survey to understand the causes of heart disease in the population. The results were eye-opening: alongside infectious diseases, there was a rising prevalence of heart disease and risk factors. This groundbreaking survey brought recognition, and I was awarded the gold medal, the highest honor for being the youngest researcher in Pakistan, by the Pakistan Academy of Medical Sciences, akin to the National Academy of Medicine in the U.S. This project paved the way for further studies and improvements in health care and treatment in Pakistan.

In recognition of my research potential, in 2001, I received a Fulbright scholarship from the Aga Khan Foundation in Ontario, Canada, to pursue a master's degree in Epidemiology and Community Health, particularly focusing on heart disease in Pakistan. The scholarship covered all expenses and provided a stipend.

Sunita Dodani with classmates during MSc at Dalhousie University, Halifax, Nova Scotia, Canada

I was admitted to Dalhousie University in Halifax, Nova Scotia, for a two-year master's program of study. My first year was spent completing coursework, and in the second year, I authored a thesis on understanding heart diseases in the Pakistani population. Despite several falls due to the icy and snowy conditions in Halifax, I haven't suffered any fractures to date, and I enjoyed my experience. The pain of excessive walking and activities related to studying was manageable, and I adjusted my attitude over time, convincing myself that I had no special needs and was as normal as anyone else. But I also reminded myself daily that I couldn't be superwoman every day and needed to capture negative thoughts, replacing them with positive ones. Despite my challenges with polio, I fulfilled my dreams, and wouldn't let polio stop me from achieving my career goals. My heartfelt thanks go to the unwavering support of my family, who raised me with love, courage, and hope.

Alongside supportive classmates and teachers, I completed my studies in Halifax. My thesis, written in Pakistan, centered on heart disease. In 2002, I returned to Halifax to defend my thesis and was awarded my degree. After graduation, I returned to Pakistan to continue my work at AKU as an assistant professor. Before earning my master's degree, I was 80 percent involved in clinical work and patient care. However, after acquiring research skills, I was allocated 30 percent of my time to develop projects, write grants, and work with underserved communities through research initiatives. This new focus allowed me to climb the ladder of success and grow as a physician-scientist.

In 2002, during a medical conference in Montreal, Canada, Dr. Ron La-Porte, and Dr. Luke Culler from the University of Pittsburgh approached me with an offer to join them, earn a PhD, and receive a second Fulbright scholarship. Although I had already received one Fulbright, they assured me I was eligible for another. This was a major honor to collaborate with these well-renowned researchers. In 2002-03, I decided to pursue this opportunity and informed my parents of my plans to return to the U.S. for a doctorate in epidemiology. Initially hesitant, they understood my desire to learn more. While Dr. LaPorte and his team were working on my student visa, Dr. LaPorte gave me a task to create a network of physicians in Pakistan, called Super-course. The University of Pittsburgh provided a stipend to establish Super-course, a digital network for physicians to exchange knowledge and medical education. This role required extensive travel across all four provinces of Pakistan. I traveled alone, meeting numerous colleagues, and making new friends while disseminating crucial health information that had the potential to save lives. My journeys often took me to rural areas in northern Pakistan, traveling by car. I was determined to overcome any challenge and accomplish my goals. During those travels, I met Dr. Suman Yazdani in Lahore and Dr. Shabina Raza in Peshawar (northern Pakistan). They became good friends. The Supercourse network grew to include over 600 physicians from across Pakistan, all dedicated to sharing medical education (https://sites.pitt.edu/~super1/).

In April 2003, I accepted the second Fulbright scholarship and received my U.S. visa to work toward a PhD in Epidemiology at the University of Pittsburgh. My studies and work kept me busy, and I was grateful for the unique opportunities that came my way. Despite challenges that included polio, ulcerative colitis, anxiety, occasional self-doubt, and people's rudeness, nothing could stop me! My life changed in Pittsburgh due to not only having a wonderful mentor, Dr. LaPorte (may his soul rest in peace) - but I also got married!

CHAPTER SIX

Life After Marriage

In 2004, I married a very good-looking, intelligent, and physically normal person!

At 22 years old, I graduated from Aga Khan University (AKU) and embarked on my postgraduate education. Driven by the goal of becoming a practicing cardiologist, I worked tirelessly to achieve numerous educational milestones, managing to reduce my studies by several years. My parents shared the aspiration that I become the youngest physician with exceptional postgraduate training. However, during this intense period of academic pursuit, unexpected family pressure arose for me to marry. "She's a doctor now and should get married," many relatives insisted. Yet, despite my achievements, my grand-parents and other relatives maintained a negative attitude toward me. "So what if she has become a doctor? That will not hide her polio, and nobody will marry her," remarked my step-grandmother.

In our culture, parents, elders, and relatives arrange marriages. Unlike my sister, I did not receive any decent marriage proposals. Some of my father's good friends were supportive and helped my parents search for a suitable match for me. However, none of the proposals my parents received met their standards. Most of these offers came from a place of sympathy. Neighbors and family friends suggested my parents lower their expectations and compromise to find me a match, but my mother was adamant that, given my elevated level of education, my match should be equivalent.

As a result, the proposals I received from Hindu families in Pakistan were often from elderly or disabled men or those looking for a second wife. These were considered "good enough" by family relatives, but not by my parents. Despite my mother's determination to find a suitable match for me, I could see worry and hopelessness in her eyes. They were also concerned about my future, especially how I would cope if I remained single into old age.

Their worry and stress affected me. Despite being young, good-looking, educated, and earning a good income, it was still not enough to overshadow my polio or make families overlook it. I thought by pursuing a successful career, I had alleviated my parents' worries, but perhaps I had not.

At AKU, both the faculty and students were open-minded. I felt valued and appreciated. Senior male students, with their enlightened attitudes, were respectful and showed interest in me, though it was unclear if their families would support me as a marriage choice. I often felt "the public doesn't know my value." Moreover, these men were Muslims, while we were Hindus. I did not want to marry someone from a different religion and bring disgrace to my family, so I graciously refused their offers. Marrying outside our religion would have given my relatives another reason to taunt my parents, claiming they couldn't find a match within our religion and had to settle for someone from a different faith. It would suggest to the community that I rejected Hindus and that only outsiders would marry me. I was my parents' pride, and I would never let them feel ashamed of me. I believed in my family and cultural values and wouldn't marry outside our faith, which would be a huge taboo and stigma. If I were to marry, it would be with my parents' approval in an arranged marriage. If not arranged by my family, any marriage proposal would still need to be approved by my parents.

When I came to the U.S. for preventive cardiology training in 1999, at the University of Colorado – Denver, I discovered matrimonial websites exclusively for Indians, Muslims, and other special interest groups. This gave hope to my parents and me, as it meant marriage options were not limited to the small number of Hindu families in Pakistan. Since by then I was 29 years old and unmarried, my parents were particularly concerned about what would happen to me if they passed away. My sister Sarla and our older brother Suresh were already married.

My brother Roop, who lived in Boulder, and I were both unmarried and remained close. Being a very obedient and caring son, Roop started looking for matches for me on the matrimonial sites as well as within his friend circle in the U.S. I also explored those sites for suitable matches in the U.S. The search was not easy.

In Pakistan, due to low literacy and cultural norms, Hindu families prefer beautiful and physically fit girls for their sons. It doesn't matter if the sons have mental or physical problems or are financially unstable; the girl must be lovely and physically normal. Education is considered secondary. Even today, only a few Hindu families are open to accepting people with disabilities. For professional women like me, who continue their education to the postgraduate level, marrying in their thirties is considered normal. However, my parents came from a background where girls married in their early twenties.

In my culture, parents would consider local youth as possible marriage partners. But I was independent and beyond that approach. I was becoming more assertive with leadership skills in communication as an outgoing person. Having been born with a spirit of independence and justice, I would fight for my rights and those of others. Unlike many young women in our culture, I was not submissive. Even with polio, I never felt guilt about my condition (why should I?) until others told me I didn't deserve to live, succeed, or be happy. Community influence tried to subjugate me to male authority like the other women.

In 2000, while in Nova Scotia, Canada, working on a master's degree at Dalhousie University, I continued occasionally browsing matrimonial websites. One person from Canada contacted me via email and showed interest. I, for a moment, was happy that somebody from the same religion, single, and a decent person had shown interest. We chatted for some time. He had his own business and eventually shared that he wanted to marry me and didn't care about my polio. I did get attracted to him. He genuinely liked me as a person, and my heart said this might be it - no more soulmate searching by my family would be required. When I arrived in Halifax, I invited him to come over during my brother Roop's visit. At the time, he disclosed that he was married and would be getting a divorce. I certainly was disappointed, but then I appreciated his frankness when our relationship could have gone beyond friendship.

When chatting online with new acquaintances, I was upfront about being a polio survivor. Some young men, particularly doctors, understood; others did not. Many stopped chatting after learning about my condition. I explored only the profiles of Hindu, unmarried, and professional men, especially doctors, IT professionals, and business professionals. Meetings with those who were still interested after learning about my polio were arranged in the presence of a family member or a friend for safety reasons.

I offered to meet some candidates at the events I traveled to in the U.S. Most were young Indian men who had immigrated to the U.S. or were Indian Americans. After meeting in person, there was often no follow-up, and I understood. Although their indifferent attitudes hurt, I now realize it happened for a good reason. There were a few whom I rejected after meeting, sensing they were more interested in my income and potential future earnings than me as an attractive wife and companion.

I recall a man from Tampa, Florida, who was interested in marrying me. However, I couldn't shake the feeling that his interest, like that of a few others, was driven by my lucrative career as a doctor. It's often difficult to discern the integrity of someone you've just met. I needed a sincere and dependable husband, as I was getting older and wanted to raise a child. Not a single matrimonial proposal reached fruition.

On a positive note, I reconnected with many AKU classmates and met new people during those visits to the U.S., who remain among my best friends to this day: Jairaj from Chicago, Naveen from New Jersey, and Rashid from Virginia, along with Christine, my schoolmate and lifelong friend. These individuals are pillars of support, always ready to help in times of need.

In 2002, after receiving a master's degree from Canada, I became an Assistant Professor at AKU, advancing in my career. My father had retired from his government job. My mother, suffering from osteoarthritis, was not doing well. I was 32, then 33, and my mother became increasingly worried about my future, hoping I would find my soulmate.

My second Fulbright scholarship came in 2002, and I was thrilled to be joining the University of Pittsburgh the following year for my PhD work. I made trips to Pakistan to establish Supercourse, an Internet-based network of healthcare professionals. During that time, and before I departed for Pittsburgh in February 2003, I met online and chatted with Arvin (my subsequent husband) on a matrimonial website.

Arvin is from India and came to the U.S. in 1996 to pursue a master's in computer science from Illinois State University in Bloomington, Illinois. He comes from a middle-class family, and his father gave him only $2000 for his graduate coursework. Arvin worked several jobs to pay for his tuition and living costs. Financially, his background was like that of my family. He has two sisters and was surprised, like many others, to learn about Hindus in Pakistan. Many people assume that after the partition in 1947, all Hindus in Pakistan moved to India, but that wasn't the case. Today, more than 50,000 Hindus live in Pakistan, in and around Sindh Province.

During our initial conversations online, I informed Arvin about my polio and what I physically could and couldn't do. An IT professional rather than a doctor, Arvin asked questions about being a Hindu and having polio in Pakistan. Out of curiosity, he asked if I could walk, and I responded, "Not only can I walk fast, but I can also run and climb stairs." To my pleasant surprise, my polio did not affect his interest at all. He was impressed that I could run. He mentioned that he wanted to marry a doctor because he hoped to engage in charitable medical work in India.

I explained that was why I had become a doctor, too, because my mother had wanted me to help children in need without supportive families.

We clicked. He said, "I don't care if you have polio or cancer; I want to marry you."

I told him if my parents approved, we would marry, but if not, we wouldn't. He has a spiritual guru (Arvin told me after marriage). He had met several girls – and even drove 16 hours to get acquainted with one of them. He used to tell his guru about every girl he met, and his guru said about each one: "She's not for you." Arvin told his guru about me – "She's from Pakistan, a doctor, and has polio." His guru said, "She's the one."

When we started chatting, he was working at Twin Tower, New York, and lived in New Jersey in an apartment with a few colleagues from India. As more information was exchanged, the prospect of our marriage grew more promising.

I informed Roop and my parents about Arvin so they could conduct a background check on his family and their status in India. Arvin's parents lived in a rural town. He is the only son, with two sisters—one of whom lived in India at the time but now resides in South Carolina. His father held a government position, and Arvin was the only one from his family to move to the U.S. According to my father, Arvin's parents were humble and simple people. I explained to Arvin about my Fulbright scholarship at the University of Pittsburgh and that I would be in Pittsburgh around April 2003. I also mentioned my parents would be visiting, along with Roop.

When I arrived in Pittsburgh, my parents came to see me in August 2003. Arvin drove from New Jersey to Pittsburgh, and that was when I met him in person for the first time. My parents liked him immediately. His honesty, simplicity, and straightforwardness impressed everyone.

He spoke from the heart. With our families' consent, we got married on January 28, 2004. It was a modest gathering with ninety to a hundred people, mainly my father's college friends who had moved to the U.S., and my classmates. Our relatives and friends in Pakistan did not attend due to visa issues. Jairaj and Christine also attended the wedding, adding to my joy. Our wedding was beautiful and lasted two days. Some Hindu weddings go for seven days – thankfully, not ours.

Sunita Dodani with husband Arvin at their wedding reception

Our wedding was the first meeting with my in-laws. I could see they were not happy, but they accepted Arvin's wishes. He had informed them he would marry me and no one else. I understood about his being the only son – the parents had big plans for him: a beautiful girl in normal health to address their needs as well as their son's.

The first year was rough. His parents stayed with us for the first three months. I didn't understand their language as they spoke Punjabi, and I spoke Sindhi. Their way of living was different; my father was cultured, and we never used curse language at home. For Arvin's family, cursing was normal, and it was uncomfortable for me. At first, several issues had to be navigated. However, I was ready to adjust and be considerate. Many times, after seeing the unhappiness of my mother-in-law, I told Arvin he shouldn't have married me out of pity. He said, "No, I didn't."

I said to him, "Look at your parents." Their attitude was often disapproving. They overlooked my medical degree, my doctorate, my master's degree, and my lifelong struggles, choosing instead to fixate on my polio. My only redeeming feature seemed to be that I was moderately good-looking. Tensions sometimes erupted. It felt like déjà vu, reminiscent of what I had endured in Pakistan with my family, relatives, and step-grandmother. But this time, it was different. I was a grown-up professional and a strong woman who could fight for anything without anybody's support and without getting hurt.

I was studying for a PhD, as well as holding a university job, and simultaneously had to take care of my in-laws' needs, prepare food for them, and get to know my husband. Every day, after finishing school, I came home to cook dinner for everyone, as my in-laws would wait for me instead of making meals themselves. I loved cooking and didn't mind despite the extra busyness. My mother-in-law (may her soul rest in peace) had expectations that her daughter-in-law would take care of her, do all the housework, and be available at any time. Every mother-in-law in India expects her daughter-in-law to care for the in-laws living in the same house. However, I was not physically able to walk fast or rush around and get groceries; I moved at my own pace. In addition to my studies, I was also working, so I was very tired. An occasional irritation was that Arvin didn't help with the house chores. Was it because of Indian culture that the bride typically does all the housework? Or did he consider me fully capable without need of assistance? That dilemma sticks in my mind even today. He would watch television while I was busy caring for the home and cooking our meals.

Despite my efforts to satisfy his family and make them happy, it didn't initially work out. Many times, I argued with Arvin about his mother not doing anything to help. I was unhappy and often questioned myself—had I made the right marriage decision?

During my stay in Pittsburgh, a family friend gave me a car. Many times when we had differences at home, especially with the in-laws, I would take the car and drive around town, not sure which bridge I was on or where I was going, and then come back. I just needed some time to consider why Arvin wasn't explaining things to his parents. I wondered why I had to make all the effort. They wanted a flawless beauty queen. He wanted a doctor and a good soul.

A few months after marriage, Arvin's sister migrated to the U.S. She, with her husband and four-year-old son, stayed with us for a few months. In India, she was a lawyer, but soon after coming to the U.S., she gave up her education and with her husband operated a minimart and a gas station in South Carolina. Anita, my sister-in-law, is truly kind, and even though she is strong-minded, she and I bonded very well. Our friendship was a welcome addition to family relationships. Even today, I cherish a beautiful relationship with her.

Expectations from both sides must be realistic. Arvin's mother eventually realized that having polio was not my fault. How often do you see a polio victim as a cardiologist, with a master's degree and a doctorate? Over time, our relational differences dissolved, and we became attached. I was the one who had to take the first step, trying to please her. She became comfortable with me, and I realized she was a good lady.

My father-in-law (may his soul rest in peace) was more resistant at first. But after his wife died in 2017, he mellowed. He always said he couldn't bring me to his culture in India because rural people wouldn't accept me. Did it hurt? Yes, I'm a human being. However, I always remembered what my father told me: "People will not change; it is you who must think above them to the level that their words should not touch you." My father-in-law's attitude did not hinder my professional growth because I am a strong woman born with leadership capabilities, which were enhanced by my parents' support and strengthened as I grew up dealing with the challenges of polio. The culture in India mirrored what I had experienced in Pakistan—the stigma was pervasive. Regardless of their flaws, people are quick to reject the limitations of others.

Similarly, marriage requires an adjustment of expectations. Like my parents, Arvin developed an affectionate attitude; he loved me and accepted me as a normal person. He didn't feel pity, only admiration. This was a valuable quality that bonded our relationship. Recognizing my sharp intellect, strong personality, leadership skills, and cheerful outlook, he and many of my friends often say if I didn't have polio, I would have been unstoppable and might have conquered the world! I still tended to fall, but I told him if I did, not to help. I wanted to get up by myself. I was brought up by my parents to be independent, and he respected that.

When we got married, Arvin didn't have a job, but we were living a comfortable life. God has always been kind to me, and he helped us through those early years. In our culture, when a daughter gets married, she receives a dowry, which includes expensive jewelry, clothes, and household furnishings given by parents to ensure their daughter has a comfortable married life. My parents and my good friend Jairaj bought us genuinely nice household furniture and other necessities. I received more than 40 expensive Pakistani dresses at the wedding. These dresses were beautiful but could only be worn on special occasions such as Indian weddings or holiday celebrations. I sold most of the dresses to my PhD classmates, who admired Pakistani clothing. My income provided financial support for my husband and my in-laws until Arvin secured employment, and I finished my PhD.

In the second year of my doctoral studies, I became pregnant with no problem. That mellowed my in-laws' behavior toward me. Somewhere might have been the thought that polio victims could not bear children. Yet, I conceived without effort.

My pregnancy was complication-free, so again I was blessed. I tend to fall, as my right leg brace doesn't bend, and therefore, by no means can I maintain constant stability. But not a single time did I fall during those nine months, even when I walked with an extra 28 to 30 pounds in the hilly area of Pittsburgh for my graduate work.

At McGee Hospital in Pittsburgh, Aneesh was delivered without complications. He was small, about 6.8 lbs. My mother came from Pakistan for a month while my mother-in-law stayed for three months to care for our small baby. He was so cute with a large face and a small body. In the first six months, he grew quickly and remained healthy. I was pleased. In our culture, girls are not appreciated in the same way as boys. When a daughter marries, she will join her husband's family, but the son will carry forward the ancestral name. I'm blessed to have a child, especially a son, which made the in-laws particularly happy. Arvin took diligent care of me when his parents returned to India.

I realized that I had a beautiful life. I never felt disabled or worried that people would make fun of me. There's a stark difference between living in Pakistan versus the U.S. No one here cared how I walked. Sometimes I would meet a smiling face; some might stop and say, "You are such a strong woman." In Pakistan, people just laugh at your walk, so condescending. I wanted to remain in this country, Arvin too. I submitted my naturalization application under the "Outstanding and Exceptional Researcher" category, which came through within a year. My husband was extended citizenship through me.

I went back to work a month after giving birth as my goal was to finish the PhD in three years. I took up my book bag and caught a bus or walked uphill to the university. Between classes, I pumped milk and carried the heavy bag home again. Then Arvin went to India to visit his parents, and I took care of Aneesh and myself during his absence. We started Aneesh's daycare at the age of four months, and he did fine. Though I came to Pittsburgh to complete my PhD, I never severed ties with AKU. I maintained my faculty appointment as an Assistant Professor in the Department of Family Medicine, with a joint appointment in the Cardiology Division of the Department of Internal Medicine. I took an extended, unpaid educational leave to focus on my PhD to return to AKU and continue my work in Pakistan.

However, my plans changed during the second year of my PhD studies when I got married. My husband, Arvin, is from India, and due to the ongoing tensions between India and Pakistan, it was not feasible for us to return to either country. Although India and Pakistan have been separate nations since 1947, the political and social strains persist. Arvin's father, like mine, held a government position, making relocation to a country viewed as an adversary impractical. Consequently, both our families decided it was best for us to marry and settle in the U.S.

I remain deeply grateful to AKU for the opportunities provided, which allowed me to develop as a distinguished doctor with numerous credentials. It was important to me to give back to AKU. In the final year of my PhD program, in collaboration with my AKU cardiology mentor, Dr. Kazmi, I organized a research training workshop at AKU in 2005. I assembled a team of U.S. trainers from the University of Pittsburgh, including my mentor, Dr. Ron LaPorte, his wife, Dr. Jan Dorman (a researcher), Dr. Thomas Songer (an epidemiologist), and Dr. Rahbar Hussian, a former AKU faculty member who returned to the U.S. after 9/11. This significant research training workshop on improving heart health was held at AKU and was video telecast to two other universities in Pakistan. My AKU mentors and the leadership were appreciative of this initiative but were saddened by the news that I would not be returning to Pakistan. They understood my legitimate reasons for staying in the U.S. and were pleased with my marriage and the accomplishments I had achieved.

True to plan, I finished my PhD in three years in 2006, and I joined the faculty in the Department of Internal Medicine at the University of Pittsburgh Medical Center (UPMC). This was a new chapter of my career as a trained healthcare professional, which was quite different from what I had faced in Pakistan.

Sunita Dodani receiving PhD degree at the graduation ceremony,
University of Pittsburgh, Pittsburgh, PA

Arvin secured an IT position at the same university doing work
that he enjoyed. We settled into our new roles comfortably with high
hopes for the future.

CHAPTER SEVEN

A Journey of Resilience

In this chapter of my life, I learned the importance of resilience and the strength needed to overcome adversity. While the journey was fraught with challenges, it also underscored the significance of focusing on the positive influences in our lives and rising above those who seek to bring us down.

After completing my PhD, my professional career in the U.S. began at UPMC. It was deeply gratifying to return to my faculty role after three years as a student. While being a PhD student was an enriching experience, I felt a strong urge to resume faculty duties. Now, with two doctorates, I was thrilled to be back on my career path as a physician epidemiologist.

Although my first job post-PhD was at UPMC, I was actively seeking senior-level positions to demonstrate my leadership and administrative skills. I have always been a natural leader, blessed with a sharp and intelligent mind, and I was eager to take on roles that would allow me to highlight and further develop these abilities.

Just one month after starting at UPMC, I accepted the position of Dean of Research and assistant professor at a medical college in Georgia. In this new role, I collaborated closely with the school of nursing, marking my first experience outside of Pakistan working with and training nurses as nurse scientists. I thoroughly enjoyed this job, gaining new leadership skills and actively participating in the leadership team. My role involved extensive travel, attending, and presenting at numerous scientific meetings.

During my tenure, I traveled nationally and internationally, including to the World Health Organization (WHO) in Geneva for a leadership workshop. Although I was always hardworking, I often worked 18-hour days to demonstrate the impact a physician-scientist could have on healthcare and disease management. I left clinical practice to focus on research, building my leadership and research expertise. My work on improving heart disease outcomes in U.S. minorities gained recognition, and within three years, I secured over $5 million in federal grants for the medical college. My supervisor was pleased with my performance, and I had staunch support from everyone at the institution. I not only advanced my career but also trained doctors, nurses, and allied healthcare professionals in clinical research. In two years, I was promoted to Associate Professor level.

I cherished this period of my life, enjoying time with Arvin and watching Aneesh grow. Despite his tiny birth size, Aneesh quickly became a healthy, chubby toddler who was attached to me. We had good friends who supported and hosted our visits. I often reminded myself that this was my true world, where I was valued and respected, free from the degradation and humiliation I had faced due to having polio. Despite the long hours, frequent solo travels, and home chores, including taking care of Aneesh, I never felt tired. My ulcerative colitis, an autoimmune disease, was also improving and remained in remission with medication, without the need for steroid boosts. There were no relapses, and my incontinence gradually improved. I incorporated home remedies, such as aloe vera juice, which significantly helped manage my condition. I was mindful of my health and constantly reminded myself that with both polio and ulcerative colitis, I needed to balance my work and family life. However, this was easier said than done. Being a workaholic with a strong drive to advance in my career, my balance often tipped more towards work.

Arvin became interested in golf due to the Masters tournament in Georgia, and occasionally our son, Aneesh, accompanied him to this exciting event. But later, Aneesh also got interested in golf and started participating in several tournaments at the school level and brought home several awards.

After three and a half years, I was offered a senior position as Associate Professor and Founding Director of a research center at a medical university in Kansas. I also negotiated a secure job for Arvin at the same university. My salary doubled from what I had earned before.

During that time, I fulfilled a promise to my mother by establishing a charitable organization called the Center for Post-Polio Rehabilitation (https://www.cfppr.org/index.html). The objective was to help children from developing countries with polio or any kind of physical disability by providing necessary medical support. I was fortunate to have supportive parents, but not every child with a disability is so lucky. Arvin fully supported my efforts and managed the center as its treasurer.

Sunita Dodani at an orphanage in India. With husband Arvin, four year old son Aneesh and CfPPR team

We traveled to India and Pakistan, visiting orphanages and elementary schools to identify children and their families in need of medical assistance. My center collaborated with local surgeons and hospitals to perform free surgeries, provide post-surgery physical therapy, and offer moral support to the families. I was able to assemble a team of dedicated healthcare professionals, including Dr. Holly Wise, a physical therapist from South Carolina, who accompanied me to India to train local physical therapists. Arvin and Aneesh accompanied us, and we provided free medical services to more than 60 children from an orphanage.

I felt immensely satisfied knowing that I was finally fulfilling my mother's goal of making me a doctor. This endeavor allowed me to give back and make a tangible difference in the lives of children with disabilities. This was my first visit to India, and although the reactions of people on the streets were like those in Pakistan, they didn't affect me. By then, I had become mentally stronger and had risen above such negativity.

In my new position as the center director, I built the research center from scratch, and it brought in significant funding. My center and I were receiving considerable attention and I developed innovative ideas to build the infrastructure of research within the institution. My supervisor supported me, but soon, after the recruitment of a new cardiology head, friction surfaced with the head of cardiology and a few others as the center began attracting widespread interest. I was training physicians as researchers and was awarded funding for the community engagement work. Animosity arose in the medical school. Some colleagues and associates made me feel uncomfortable with their attitudes toward me, and I felt as if I had been cornered for criticism, which differed hugely from the South. Although the beginning of my tenure attracted support, that dwindled. As public interest grew in the new research center, collegial encouragement waned, though I was expecting the opposite, i.e., I would be showered with encouragement and assistance. I was not able to understand this different attitude of colleagues.

Nevertheless, I continued working hard at my job. I continued my growth at the international level by participating and presenting at international meetings in Hawaii, Brazil, Turkey, and many more. Sometimes Arvin and Aneesh came with me. Those experiences were enjoyable as I presented the findings of our research and continued to develop my professional career as a cardiovascular researcher. Despite getting tired at times, I tried to make the most of each day. Polio never intervened. When flights got canceled, I would stay at an airport for hours and hours, like any traveler, without compromising my work or personal needs. Every month brought a trip, sometimes two trips. When not traveling, attending scientific meetings, and leading a busy life, I would get home by eight or nine p.m. Determination kept me going.

Sunita Dodani at a national conference in Washington DC

One day, the head of cardiology said to me, "Why are you working? You have polio; you should stay at home." He added, "I'm surprised that you are married and were able to give birth to a child. Is he really your child or adopted?" All through my life, my mantra has been to focus on work and never say anything to anyone who may hurt someone's feelings. I learned this from my parents and have witnessed it during my lifetime. What goes around comes around. For a second, I looked around and patted myself to make sure I wasn't back in Pakistan. I was surprised to hear this from an educated person, who I had supported during his transition period and spent hours with him to discuss collaborative work. Was this déjà vu'? A thought came to me to report him to human resources, but I instead mentioned it to my supervisor. Sadly, he did not take any action. Later, I understood that this person wanted to take over the center that I had built from the ground up. While there were no other grounds to pin me down, he attacked me personally. His apparent envy was disconcerting. But maybe God wanted me to meet all kinds of people and learn to adapt. I didn't understand the department head's dismissive remarks about polio, echoed by a few others. I reminded myself to stay strong: "I have faced this so often. Nothing is going to significantly shake me."

The situation worsened when my support team was turned against me - my staff, researchers, study coordinators, and others. I didn't know what was happening behind my back. The insidious plot was to remove me from this position and replace me. The enemies criticized my research and made false accusations, inciting an investigation. Everything came out clean when evidence was requested, and no wrongdoing was found. But their accusations shook me; it was hard to understand that trusted colleagues and staff would make false claims about my work. When everything came to light, I confronted my supervisor and said, "If you wanted to give my center to someone else, you should have just told me directly. Why go through all this, attacking me personally and professionally?" Further, I said, "You should have told me to surrender the position to the head of cardiology. I would have given it to him instead of being confronted by false accusations." He had no response. I resigned immediately, but the entire ordeal had a profound impact on me.

I had always believed that bullying and unfair treatment were behaviors of uneducated people in developing countries and that such things didn't happen in the U.S. However, this experience shattered that fantasy. I realized that human nature is consistent regardless of location; when it comes to taking advantage, people can stoop to any level. The location doesn't matter.

Throughout my career, only a select few have genuinely encouraged and applauded my endurance and achievements. Unfortunately, many in my profession, as in others, often react to my successes with jealousy. They might undermine what I have built and created, but they can never strip away my intellect and resilience.

At times, it felt as though I had been thrown down a mountain, left trembling and disoriented. I plunged into depression, and my unwavering belief in my resilience faltered. My health deteriorated, and I struggled with depression, a challenge made worse by my sensitivity. I had once believed that the discriminatory mindset of professional academics, unwilling to accept a woman with a disability in a professional role, was confined to developing countries like Pakistan or India. However, I learned that this mindset knows no borders. Moving from one place to another is not a solution. Those who face challenges must be strong, bold, and courageous, rising above the bar set by those who try to overshadow or hurt them.

We should focus on colleagues and friends who are supportive, who celebrate our successes, and who offer a smile of encouragement and a shoulder to cry on. Critics will always be around, whether in Pakistan, India, or the U.S. We must rise above their demeaning attitudes. When an investigation was launched and ended with negative results, I became disheartened and resigned. I no longer wanted to remain in that environment. Despite my husband's unwavering support, I experienced substantial stress. My work no longer mattered.

The unexpected criticism and condemnation broke me.

Arvin has always been supportive and said, "This happens to show not everyone is good, and God wanted you to experience it."

For several months, I remained in a state of depression, not even looking for jobs. Overwhelmed by stress, I decided to go to Pakistan to be with my mother, who had always been my beacon of light. During this time, she was diagnosed with a brain tumor, and I wanted to convince her to undergo surgery in the U.S. It was a precious period, that allowed me to be by her side and reaffirm my belief that everything happens for a reason.

In 2011, I was finally able to persuade her to have the surgery in the U.S., where most of her cancer was successfully removed.

After being with my mother during her surgery and the successful removal of her brain tumor, my confidence and natural buoyancy were restored. I began looking for employment, and we sold our house in Kansas. I accepted an Associate Professor position in Florida, determined to step back from leadership roles due to the devastating effects of the Kansas experience.

Arvin continued his job in Kansas, while I moved to Florida with our five-year-old son, Aneesh, who was ready to start kindergarten. For six months, Arvin and I lived apart, as he didn't have a job in Florida yet. During this time, Aneesh and I lived alone, with Arvin visiting every three to four weeks for the weekend. Initially, I didn't know many people in Florida, but one of Aneesh's school teachers, Ms. Jane Moore, was incredibly helpful. She understood how challenging it can be for a working woman (in my case, a polio survivor) with a small child to move to a new place without knowing anyone. The new job kept me busy, but I couldn't shake off the lingering impact of my Kansas sojourn. For six months, I felt like a single mom, managing a full-time job, house chores, and taking care of Aneesh with minimal support.

My primary goal was to ensure that Aneesh had everything he deserved. His school was new, and it was a fresh experience for him. I made it a point to be present at every school function, whether it was a class-related event or an extracurricular activity. Despite my exhaustion, I never made excuses to miss any of Aneesh's school activities. I ensured he participated in sports, arts, and other extracurricular programs.

Although our rented house was large, Aneesh and I found comfort in the smallest room. Every morning, I took care of him, dropped him off at school, brought him back, prepared food, and spent quality time with him. While this dedication was fulfilling, it came at the cost of my failing health.

Weekdays were hectic. I spent weekends with Aneesh, taking him to the temple and fun places he enjoyed. During this period, I neglected my health, becoming very weak. The stress of the new job, coupled with the memories of Kansas and my duties as a single mom, impacted my health. I became pale, my hair thinned, and I lost a significant amount of weight.

Jane took care of me after school, cooking meals and looking after Aneesh. We became good friends and have stayed in touch ever since. A few years ago, I visited her in Florida, and our bond remains strong to this day.

Stress is a major risk factor for many illnesses, including autoimmune diseases. Its impact on health cannot be overstated. Living just 30 minutes from the Mayo Clinic, I decided to seek medical help there. After undergoing several tests, I was diagnosed with lupus —another autoimmune illness.

My condition deteriorated rapidly. A blood transfusion became necessary as I wasn't eating properly, yet I was still trying to care for my son and maintain my job. My hemoglobin levels dropped, and I lost 50 pounds. It became too much to manage on my own. To control the disease, doctors prescribed steroids again, after 25 years.

Seeing my worsening health, Arvin left his job in Kansas and joined us. During our marriage, he had always seen me as a strong, healthy, energetic, and fun-loving person with a strong immune system. He knew that the main culprit of my sickness was stress due to an unacceptable experience in Kansas. Despite his presence, I often lost hope and felt overwhelmed by life. I frequently questioned why I had to endure so much suffering and wondered why God was so cruel as if I hadn't already endured enough pain. But Arvin gave me continued strength and said, "This is God's way of teaching you that there are all kinds of people and you should not doubt your capabilities. Don't let go of your skills— fight back."

Slowly, Arvin's constant reinforcement gave me courage. He helped me see that it wasn't my loss but rather an experience to learn from, making me stronger and more careful of the people around me. I knew I had to overcome the constant sadness. My outlook improved, and I regained control of myself. I realized that as a mentally strong woman, I couldn't let someone hurt me to the extent that it eroded my confidence. That day, I promised myself that no matter what happened, I would never let others shake me, bully me, or use my polio as a weapon to bring me down.

We spent six-and-a-half years in Florida, where we made great friends, and life gradually returned to normal. Dr. Gurjit Kaeley, a rheumatologist, became a good friend and my physician. I had the honor of mentoring him in his research career. I enjoyed my work training physicians and making considerable progress both in my professional and personal life. Aneesh was growing fast, and I cherished spending time with him.

Within three years, I received an offer to join the Mayo Clinic, where I met exceptional colleagues who valued my intellect, sharp mind, and potential. It was an honor to work at such a prestigious institution.

After more than six years in Florida and while at the Mayo Clinic, a recruiter reached out to me with an enticing leadership opportunity in Virginia. The role involved establishing an institute in partnership with a medical school and a healthcare system. The President of the medical school was seeking a visionary leader like me to build and lead the institute.

Initially, I responded with "No" because I was apprehensive about facing a repeat of my experience in Kansas, where the center I built was unprofessionally taken away from me. However, I soon realized that Virginia genuinely wanted me for this role. Why ignore leadership opportunities because of one bad incident? My skills and experience were needed to build a major new institute, and I decided to give my lifelong leadership abilities another chance. During my first visit, I was greeted warmly at the airport by the President and Vice Dean of the medical school.

Embracing the opportunity, and after receiving an exceptional offer as the Institute Director and full Professor of Medicine, I returned with full force as a leader and administrator, and we moved to Virginia in 2017.

Sunita Dodani – a strong leader

With substantial support from both the medical school and the health-care system, I built the institute from the ground up. I recruited some of the finest faculty and staff, and within five years, elevated the institute to a national level, making it a role model. I was well-respected by the majority, and during my tenure in Virginia, I made wonderful friends such as Cynthia Romero, Anca Dobrain, Beverly Roberts, Elias Siraj, Rehan Qayyum, Vanessa Hill, and many others. My supervisor and President, Dr. Richard Homan, was extremely supportive and embraced me with high respect. My administrative staff, particularly Carter Overton, provided invaluable support for many of the institute's activities.

Despite facing discrimination from a few individuals, including a cardiologist who disapproved of me from the outset due to my race and disability, I remained undeterred. My determination to display strong leadership and elevate the institute to several notches in the scientific world was unwavering. Alongside my friend Naveen, I organized a heart health conference in New Jersey, which we co-hosted. I also established a regional health coalition and with great teams, organized a conference in Toronto on mental health; I also achieved numerous other scientific accomplishments. My curriculum vitae is filled with honors, accolades, and achievements, reflecting my successful and impactful career. Aneesh was growing by leaps and bounds, excelling in his studies and golf. Now in high school, he had become a sensible teenager. Though he remained extremely attached to me, he sometimes questioned, "Ma, why do you have polio? Why couldn't I have a normal mother?" I had no answer for him.

As Aneesh became a senior in high school, I sensed he was uncomfortable introducing me to his classmates because of my polio, even though he never explicitly said so. I noticed he avoided having me meet his friends whenever I came to his school. I understood that, as a teenager, he was navigating a challenging phase and would eventually mature and gain a deeper understanding. Despite this, Aneesh always relied on me more than Arvin and knew that for anything, I would fulfill his needs. Whenever he didn't want to take the school bus, he would call and say, "Ma, can you pick me up?" Without hesitation, I would drive to his school.

To avoid making him uncomfortable in front of his friends, I refrained from attending school events, including his high school graduation ceremony—a proud moment for any parent. My happiness stemmed from knowing he was happy.

Aneesh with his father – high school graduation

As he has grown older, Aneesh now realizes and feels immensely proud of me. Looking back, I understand that he always cared for me deeply, even if he sometimes wished for a mother who wasn't affected by polio.

Sunita Dodani with parents, brother Roop and his family in Boulder, CO

My parents were always happy and proud of me. My father had hoped I would become a full professor at a young age, and I did, achieving the rank of Full Professor of Medicine in Virginia at the age of forty-six. Around the same time we moved to Virginia, my father decided to visit the U.S., staying with my brother Roop in Boulder, Colorado.

While my parents had been frequent visitors, this trip was different as only my father made the journey. Despite being seventy-five years old, he had always been in good health, maintaining a daily three-mile walk. However, during this visit to see Roop, he contracted a severe respiratory infection while on a plane. Hospitalized and losing half of his lung, he was urgently airlifted to Virginia to be by my side. It was in my Virginia home that he passed away, on the very day of my birth, after gifting me with the precious last ten days of his life. I was sad but stayed strong as that is what my parents wanted from me.

My father maintained my health file on polio from 1972. He had meticulously taped papers to the file, including my doctor's appointments, diagnosis, and relevant information. He always kept his file in his briefcase and always brought it with him to the U.S., as he believed there would be a cure for polio, and one day I would be normal. It breaks my heart and brings me to tears to think of my late father looking at this file, blaming himself, when it wasn't his fault at all. The file is now with me.

My mother, although now cancer-free, struggled with severe arthritis in her knees. While my father was alive, she refused to undergo knee replacement surgery. However, shortly after he passed away, she decided to have both knees replaced at Aga Khan University (AKU) in Pakistan. In 2019, her surgery went very well, but she went into shock (sepsis) post-surgery and passed away. I was still in transit to Pakistan and learned about her death while sitting at the New York airport, waiting to board my flight. Losing both parents within two years was incredibly devastating. Everything I am today is because of them. However, I did not let depression overshadow my success but continued moving forward, knowing this is what my parents would have wanted.

My institute work was blossoming and despite COVID hitting in 2020, I did not slow down. The news of the institute's success went viral, and even though we were well settled in Virginia, I was receiving job offers from all over, which included positions like school dean, chief medical officer, center director, and many other C-suite level leadership positions. We were happy in Virginia. Aneesh finished high school, and though he accepted his undergraduate degree at one of the universities in Virginia, he always desired and dreamed of being in and around Chicago, Illinois. One of my offers included a Center founding director position in Illinois. The leadership, particularly Dean Aiyer, admired me and valued my achievements. Seeing my humble leadership and eagerness to join them and having Aneesh's desire to be in one of the upper-tier universities in Illinois, we moved to Illinois State in 2023, and I joined as the founding director of a research center and professor of medicine. I am well respected and valued here and cherish collaborating with wonderful teams. There is also a casino where I sometimes play slot machines.

Looking back on my professional career, which began in Pakistan and brought me to the U.S., I have no regrets. Despite facing numerous challenges and experiencing an unpleasant stint in Kansas, I learned valuable lessons. Although I struggled and fell into depression, I quickly bounced back. I persevered and returned stronger. I promised myself that no matter what happened, I would never let such setbacks define me again. Jealousy and ambition from others can lead to hurtful actions, but I refuse to let them undermine my achievements. Though I once felt ashamed of that experience and even had suicidal thoughts, I now understand that such challenges are part of the journey. We should all strive to be thoughtful and persistent, rising above pettiness and focusing on growth and resilience.

CONCLUSION

Contentment and Peace

Today, at fifty-four years old, I look back on my life with a profound sense of gratitude and accomplishment. I have been happily married to Arvin for over twenty years, and our son Aneesh, now nineteen, is thriving as a sophomore at an elite university in Illinois, pursuing a career in Economics and Finance. Aneesh is my pride and joy, often telling me, "Ma, once I stand on my feet, I will not let you work and will give you all the happiness and comforts of life." His words and admiration fill me with happiness, and I have no complaints about life.

Throughout my fifty-two-year journey with polio, I have encountered and endured every conceivable hardship. Is there anything that can shake me now? Absolutely not. I am a powerful woman, and nothing can take that from me. This life journey has exposed me to the physical pains of polio, mental and psychological torment from family and relatives, bullying from the public, and envious professional colleagues who underestimated my intellectual capabilities due to my disability. Each of these experiences has made me stronger and imparted valuable life lessons. Every rejection from society taught me the superficiality of the world. Physical beauty may attract people initially, but it does not last. Sincere appreciation of a pure soul is rare, but I have been fortunate to encounter a few who saw beyond my disability. These include my parents, husband, siblings, friends, and colleagues.

Had my mother not taken a stand when I contracted polio at the age of two, I could have ended up in an orphanage, possibly not surviving. My parents' timely provision of physical therapy prevented more severe disability. My mother's decision to guide me into the medical field gave me purpose and direction. Education and continuous support from teachers, friends, and colleagues enabled me to shine as a strong woman leader. Meeting Arvin added love and companionship to my life.

Though most people I encountered (more than 90 percent) were demeaning and humiliating, the 10 percent who supported me and loved me for who I am made all the difference in shaping who I am today.

Do I have any regrets or complaints? Not really. We believe in reincarnation, and if asked if I would choose the same life again, my answer would be no—not because of polio, but because of people. Words can wound deeply, often more than any physical ailment.

Sometimes, I feel the urge to climb a mountain and scream at everyone: What was my fault in all this? I did not choose polio; it was given to me by fate. So why the hatred, shaming, and bullying? If people want to make fun, direct it to the force that created me this way. Imagine if one of your children had polio and was bullied—how would you feel?

Before concluding this book, I want to leave you a message. Now that I have overcome all the roadblocks in my life, becoming a globally renowned physician and scientist highly sought after by some of the largest health organizations in America, all while maintaining an untainted soul, people praise and support me. But where were you when I needed your support the most?

When I contracted polio, it felt like a mountain had fallen on us—financially, emotionally, and socially. Instead of offering encouragement, many friends, family members, and the public were cold and suggested my family abandon me. My mother cried every night over my condition, and my father left his job because of our situation. Until his death, he blamed himself for my polio.

I hope my story serves as a reminder to be kind to others. We all have our battles. Instead of criticizing, offer a helping hand. Look for the good in people, not just the things that make you uncomfortable.

The world can become a happier, healthier place if we work together. Let's celebrate our uniqueness and support each other on our life journeys so we can look back with pride, knowing we helped rather than hurt those around us.

www.ingramcontent.com/pod-product-compliance
Lightning Source LLC
Chambersburg PA
CBHW051232120626
46547CB00013B/1611